VIRC

August 23–Se

If everything was perfect, you would never learn and you would never grow.

✧ Beyoncé ✧

BUTTERCUP

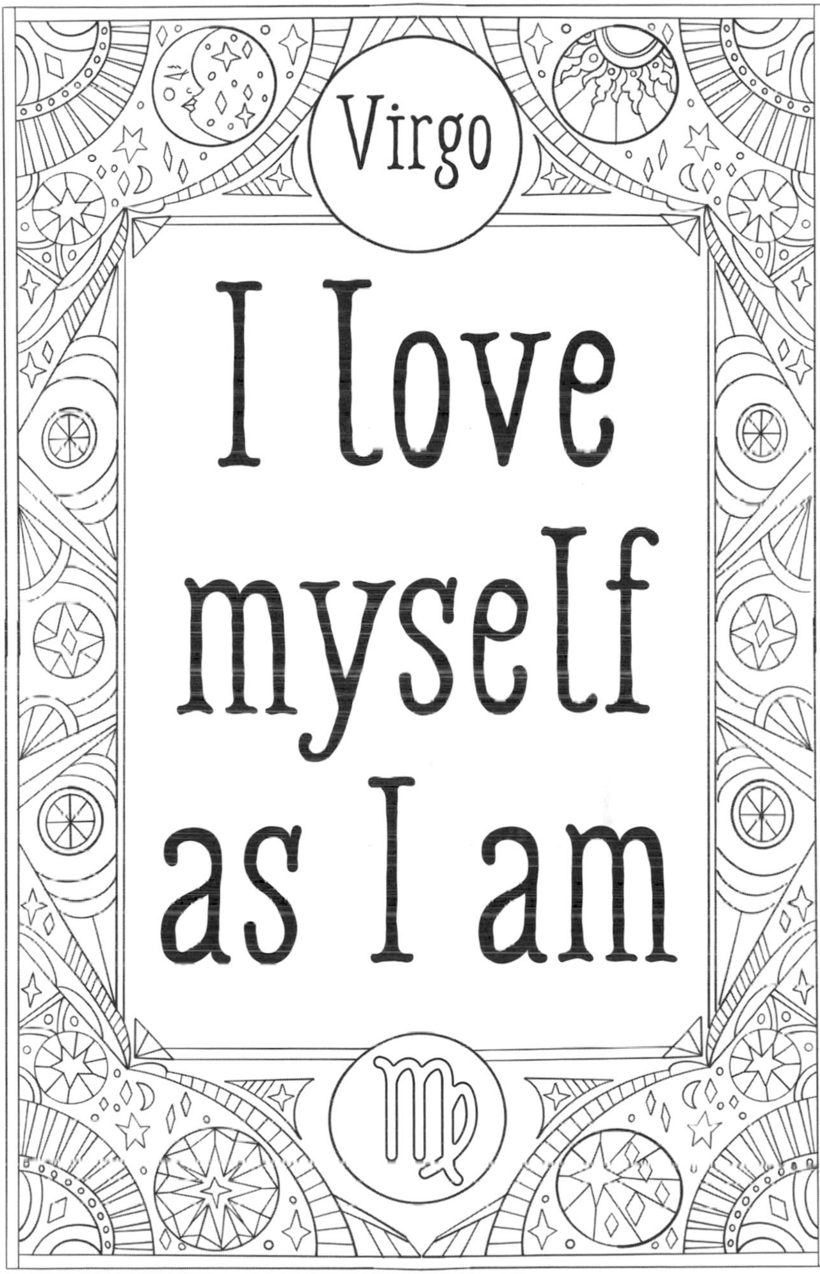
Virgo
I love myself as I am

summer

Virgo

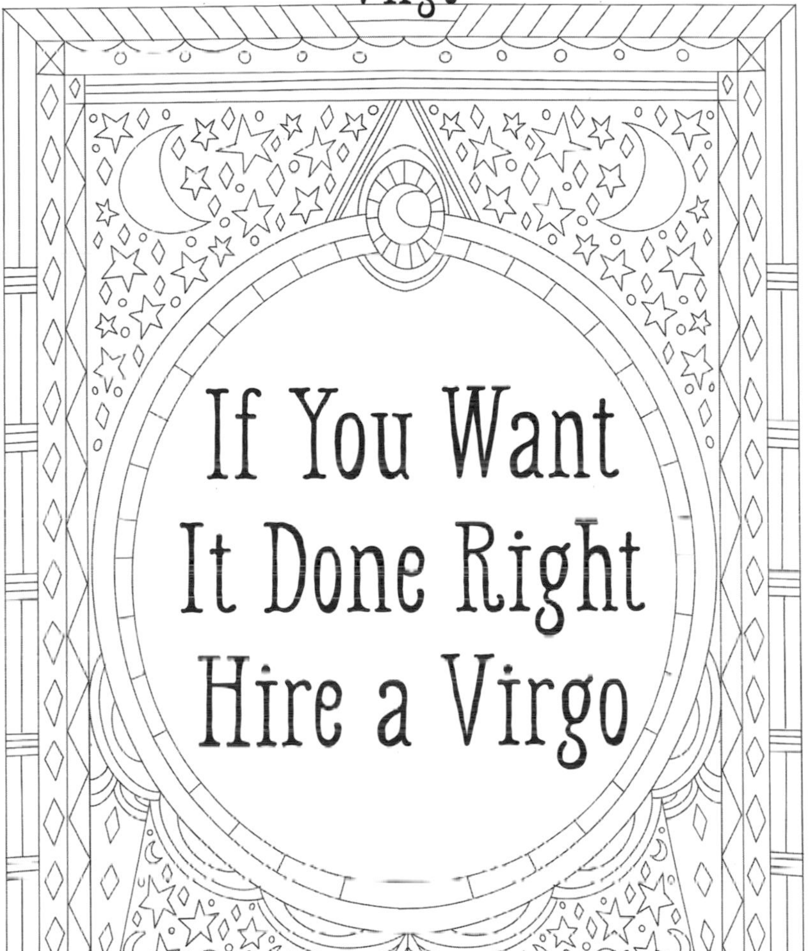

Virgo
Ruled by Mercury

Image by Andrea Lauren © Simon & Schuster, Inc.

Virgo

INTELLIGENT

Honest

Industrious

THOUGHTFUL

ADAPTABLE

RULING HOUSE
6
The House of
Health & Work

VIRGO

I respect my worth and my impact

VIRGO

Aries
Taurus
Gemini
Cancer
Leo
Virgo
Libra
Scorpio
Sagittarius
Capricorn
Aquarius
Pisces

Earth Signs
Taurus
Virgo
Capricorn

LET THE STARS LEAD THE WAY